WEATHER AND CLIMATE

SUMMER

Joy Gregory

LIGHTBOX
openlightbox.com

LIGHTBOX

Go to **www.openlightbox.com** and enter this book's unique code.

ACCESS CODE

LBXC4748

Lightbox is an all-inclusive digital solution for the teaching and learning of curriculum topics in an original, groundbreaking way. Lightbox is based on National Curriculum Standards.

STANDARD FEATURES OF LIGHTBOX

AUDIO High-quality narration using text-to-speech system

ACTIVITIES Printable PDFs that can be emailed and graded

SLIDESHOWS Pictorial overviews of key concepts

VIDEOS Embedded high-definition video clips

WEBLINKS Curated links to external, child-safe resources

TRANSPARENCIES Step-by-step layering of maps, diagrams, charts, and timelines

INTERACTIVE MAPS Interactive maps and aerial satellite imagery

QUIZZES Ten multiple choice questions that are automatically graded and emailed for teacher assessment

KEY WORDS Matching key concepts to their definitions

Contents

Splendid Summertime

An **11-year-old** boy invented the **ice pop**, a popular summer treat, in **1905**.

A **queen honeybee** lays up to **2,000 eggs a day** in summer.

The weather changes. The days are longer. The temperature is warmer. Summer is here.

Most children have a long vacation from school during summer. They spend more time outside.

What do you like to do in summer? Do you eat ice cream more often? Some families have backyard cookouts. Many children like to go to the beach or swimming pool. People play games in parks.

Most places in the United States have long hours of daylight in summer. Families may take a summer vacation. Children might go to summer camp. Imagine how your perfect summer would look.

Summer in the United States

Summer usually starts in June and ends in August. Summers are often hotter in southern states than in northern states.

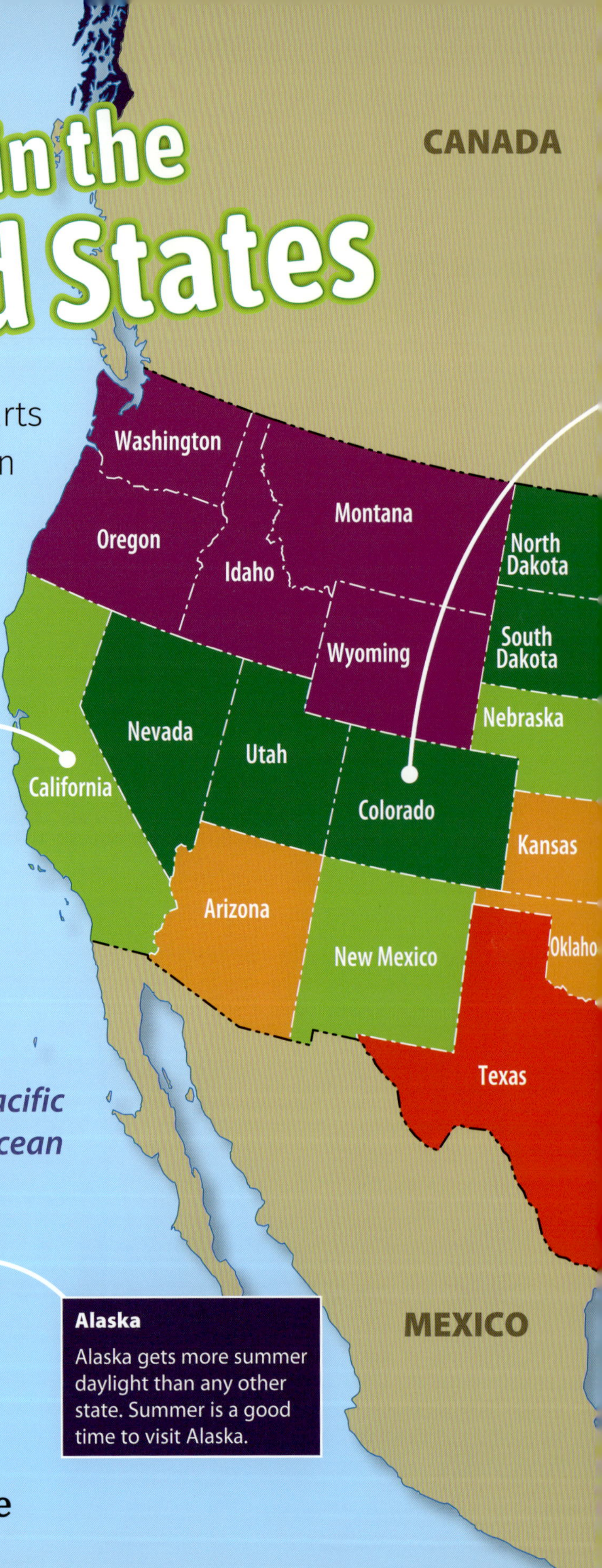

California

California holds the world record for the highest summer temperature. One day in 1913, Death Valley reached 134° Fahrenheit (57° Celsius).

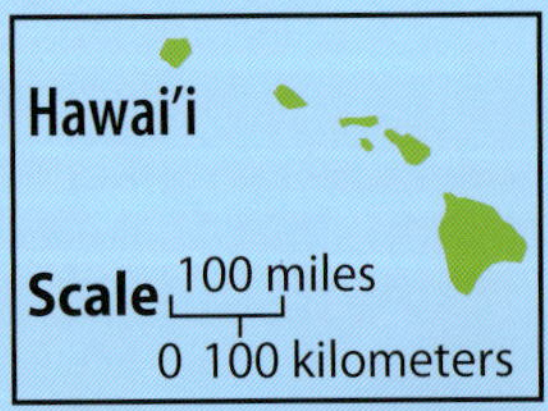

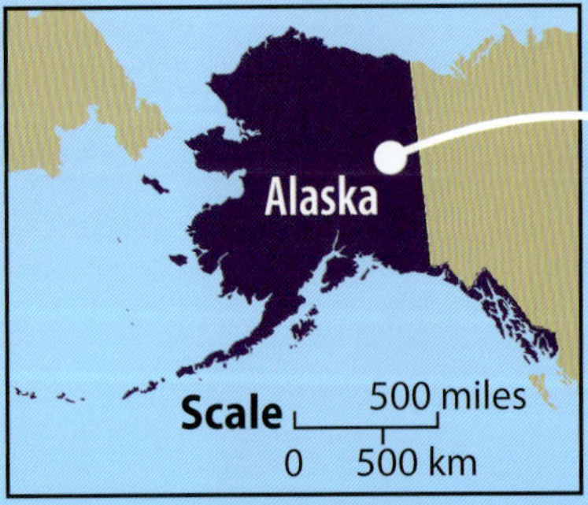

Alaska

Alaska gets more summer daylight than any other state. Summer is a good time to visit Alaska.

Colorado

Colorado has the Never Summer Mountains. Snow and ice cover them all year.

Louisiana

Louisiana has some of the hottest summers in the United States. It rains often, and the air is very **humid**.

Can You Find Your State?

Find your state on the map. What color is it? Find the same color in the legend.

What is the average temperature of your state in summer?

Legend

Degrees Fahrenheit (°F)

- 50–60
- 60–65
- 65–70
- 70–75
- 75–80
- 80–85
- Other countries
- Water

Scale 0 250 miles / 250 km

The Weather in Summer

The seasons change as Earth **orbits** the Sun. The journey takes one year. During that time, the seasons change four times. As Earth moves, part of it leans, or tips, toward the Sun. The other part leans away from the Sun.

In June, the Northern **Hemisphere** of Earth leans toward the Sun. It receives more of the Sun's heat. This is when summer begins in the United States. Summer is the warmest season of the year. This season has the most hours of sunlight. In states where summer is hot and humid, it often rains.

Summer in the Northern Hemisphere

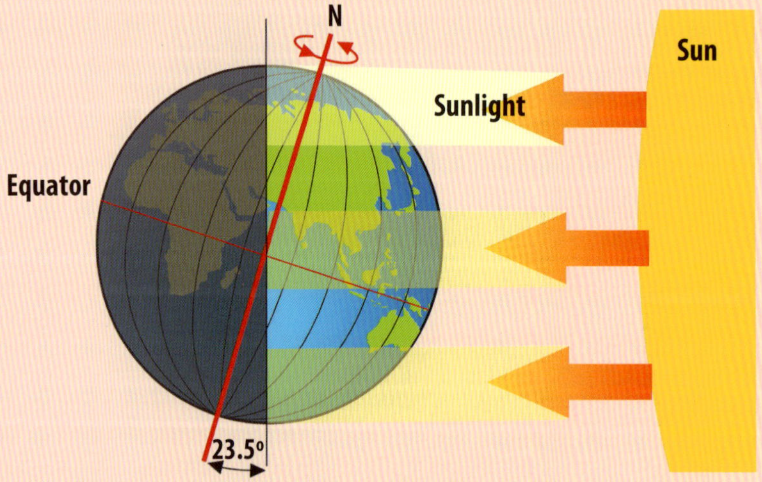

An Average Summer Season

From June to August, there are almost 850 hours of sunshine in San Diego, California.

Approximately how many hours of sunshine does Tampa get in a summer season? What about Syracuse and Dallas?

Which of these four states has the most rain in summer? Which has the least?

= 100 hours

= 1 inch (2.5 centimeters)

Nearly 1 million people were moved from their homes during the California wildfire of 2007.

Extreme Summer

Summer weather can be dangerous. High temperatures may hurt people. Too much Sun can give them **sunburn**. Humans must plan to stay safe.

HEAT WAVES

Heat waves are periods of time that are much hotter than normal. The heat may make people ill. Heat waves are worse in cities. Roads and buildings soak up more heat than land and trees.

DEHYDRATION

Hot weather causes people to sweat. Their bodies lose water. Dehydration, or a lack of water, makes people sick. Some people get headaches. Others feel dizzy or tired. They may need to go to a hospital for help.

WILDFIRES

Wildfires are more common in summer. In areas where it does not rain much, high temperatures make forests dry. Fires start easily and are difficult to control. Wildfires can damage or destroy homes.

Extreme Summer Timeline

Hot summer air brings extreme weather to the United States. Extreme summers can be very dry or full of rain and **thunderstorms**.

1930s
Year after year of **drought** causes dust storms across the United States. Crops and **livestock** die.

Summer 1980
A heat wave hits the central and eastern United States. About 10,000 people die from heat-related illnesses.

July 1990
A **hailstorm** pounds parts of Colorado. The storm causes $1.6 billion in damage.

July 1995
More than 700 Chicago residents die during a heat wave. Hospitals fill and electricity fails.

July 2014
Lightning starts four separate fires in Washington. They combine to form the Carlton Complex Fire, which burns more than 250,000 acres (101,171 hectares).

July 2018
The Mendocino Complex Fire in Northern California burns 460,000 acres (186,155 ha). It is the largest fire in state history.

Weather Tools over Time

Weather forecasters tell people what kind of weather to expect. Do you need a coat or an umbrella? Should you plant your garden? Modern technology helps **predict** the weather. Before these tools were invented, humans studied clouds. Cloud patterns helped them guess how the weather would change.

ANEMOMETER

An anemometer measures the speed of wind. Most anemometers have cups. When the wind hits the cups, the anemometer spins. Sometimes, meteorologists use wind speed to tell if a storm is coming.

Leon Battista Alberti invented the anemometer in 1450.

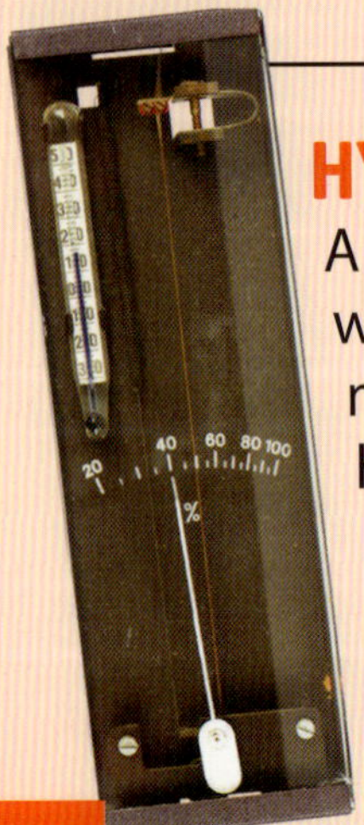

HYGROMETER

A hygrometer measures humidity. Humidity is the amount of wetness in the air. Simple hygrometers use a human hair to measure humidity. The hair expands, or gets bigger, when humidity is high. Measuring humidity helps people predict rain.

In 1783, Horace Bénédict de Saussure built the first hygrometer that used a human hair. He was a physicist and geologist.

COMPUTER WEATHER MODELS

Weather satellites collect information about temperature and cloud patterns. Scientists use the information to make computer models. The models predict the weather.

In 1950, a group of U.S. scientists proved computer-based forecasts worked. Computer scientist Klara Dan von Neumann was part of that team.

Discover Scientists

Scientists want to understand the world around us. They try to find out why things happen. You can be a scientist, too. Learn about what different kinds of scientists do.

Meteorologists study and predict the weather.

Geologists study the rocks and minerals that make up Earth.

Computer scientists write computer codes and develop software applications.

Summer Technology Today

Scientists make summer more fun. Some scientific inventions keep people safe. Other technology helps people enjoy the outdoors.

CAR SEAT SENSORS

The inside of a parked car can get too hot for children and pets. Sensors save lives. They warn drivers when a small child is left behind in a car seat.

In the United States, about 37 children die in hot cars each year.

INSULATED FOOD CONTAINERS

Insulated food containers keep food cold and safe. They come in many sizes. Some hold enough water for a hike. Others can store food for a family picnic.

Insulated food containers can keep food cold or hot. They maintain the temperature of the food that is put inside.

ELECTRIC BIKES

Electric bikes let riders go farther, faster. The motor helps the rider pedal easily. The rider is still able to get exercise. The motor helps the bike go up steep hills.

In some cities, people can rent electric bikes through smartphone apps.

A Home for a Hot Climate

Homes protect people from the **climate** where they live. In some states, summer is very hot. Other areas have hot weather all year. Houses in these places are built to help people stay safe from the heat.

Fire-resistant yards

The materials outside a home can prevent a nearby fire from spreading to the house. Rocks and cement do not catch fire. There are some trees and shrubs that do not burn easily.

Air conditioners

Air conditioners cool indoor air. They remove heat from indoor air and release the heat outdoors. Fans in air conditioners blow the cooled air back inside homes and businesses.

Blackout shades and curtains

Glass windows let energy from the Sun into a home. That energy heats the space. Blackout shades and curtains block summer sunlight. The window covers keep the inside air cool.

Non-flammable roofing

Roof fires spread quickly. The wind carries sparks to nearby buildings. Roofs made of non-flammable materials do not catch fire easily. They help prevent fires from spreading.

About **87 percent** of U.S. homes have an **air conditioner**.

Some evergreen trees **burn 5 to 10 times faster** than trees with leaves.

Sun Safety

Hot summer sunlight is dangerous. The Sun gives off ultraviolet (UV) rays of energy. These rays can harm people's eyes. They cause sunburn, which can lead to skin diseases. Heat from the Sun's rays also raises body temperature. This can make people sick. People like to be outside in summer. They should protect themselves from eye damage, sunburn, and illnesses caused by heat.

Put on sunscreen to prevent sunburn. Sunscreen should have a Sun Protection Factor (SPF) of 30 or higher.

Seek shade. The Sun's rays are strongest from 10 AM to 4 PM.

Carry a water bottle. Refill it often. Drinking plenty of water prevents dehydration.

Protect eyes from the Sun. Wear sunglasses. Wear a hat with a wide brim.

Practice Sun Safety

The Sun's UV rays may be strong or weak, depending on the time and place. A UV index is used to measure the strength of UV rays. Stay aware of the UV index at your location. This will help you stay safe from sunburn.

1. Open today's newspaper or log on to the internet. Find the forecast for your city or town. What is today's UV index?
2. Match the UV index to the chart below.
3. What should you wear to protect your skin? Do you need to seek shade between 10 AM and 4 PM? Perhaps you should stay indoors, if possible. Make a Sun safety plan that matches the UV index.

0 1 2	**Low**	
3 4 5	**Moderate**	
6 7	**High**	
8 9 10	**Very High**	
11+	**Extreme**	

Summer around the World

POLAR CLIMATE ZONE

The polar zone is the coldest climate zone. Parts of this zone are covered in ice all year. Summers are not warm in polar climates. The weather is mild and cool. There are long hours of summer sunshine.

Wildlife: Arctic Fox, Arctic Wolf, Penguin, Polar Bear

TEMPERATE CLIMATE ZONE

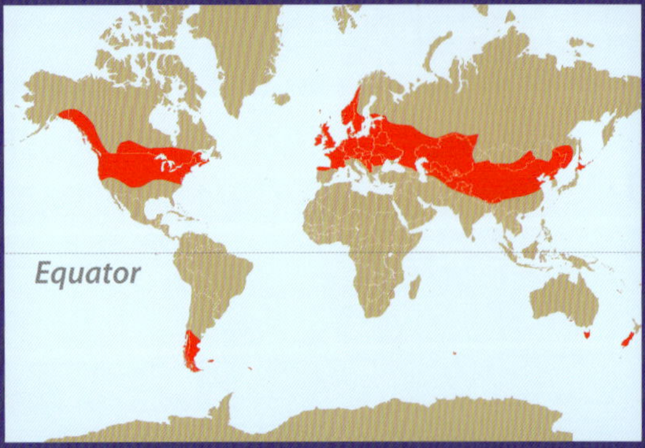

The temperate zone has four very different seasons. These are winter, spring, summer, and fall. Summers are warm in temperate zones. Summer weather changes quickly. It may be sunny, then rain soon afterward.

Wildlife: Giant Panda, Raccoon, Red Fox, Squirrel

Summer is different around the world. An imaginary line called the equator circles Earth, dividing it into two halves. Places close to the equator are often hot all year. Areas far from the equator are cold. Earth has four major climate zones.

SUBTROPICAL CLIMATE ZONE

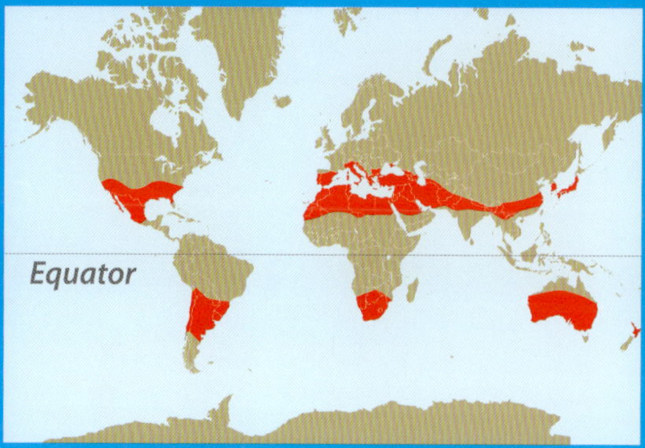

The subtropical zone has a warm or hot climate. Its two main seasons are summer and winter. Temperatures do not change very much from summer to winter. In summer, the weather is hot and dry or hot and humid.

Wildlife: Alligator, Kangaroo, Leopard, Python

TROPICAL CLIMATE ZONE

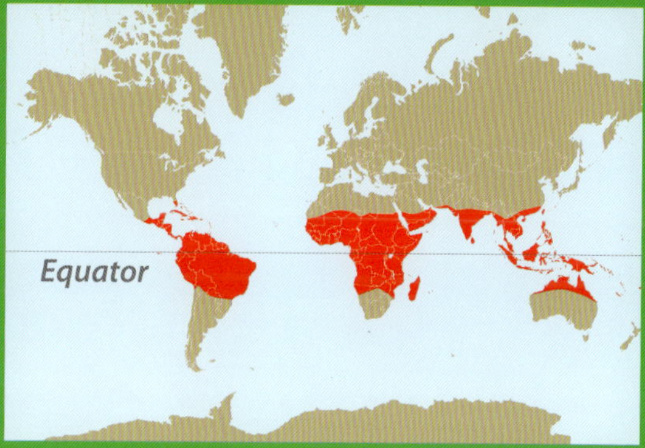

The tropical zone is the hottest climate zone. The weather is warm year-round. Many inches (millimeters) of rain fall from May to August. During that period, the average temperature is above 77°F (25°C). Some areas have heavy rain all year.

Wildlife: Gorilla, Komodo Dragon, Orangutan, Rhinoceros

Quiz

1 Which is the hottest climate zone?

A: Tropical climate zone

2 What is the name of the scientist who invented the anemometer?

A: Leon Battista Alberti

3 In which state are the Never Summer Mountains?

A: Colorado

4 What percentage of U.S. homes have an air conditioner?

A: About 87 percent

5 How many eggs can a queen honeybee lay per day in summer months?

A: Up to 2,000

6 How can you protect your eyes from sunburn?

A: Wear sunglasses and a hat with a wide brim

7 What are some common weather hazards in summer?

A: Wildfires, heatwaves, thunderstorms, and drought

8 When was the ice pop invented?

A: In 1905

9 Where was the world record for the highest summer temperature reached?

A: In Death Valley, California

10 Which state gets more daylight in summer than any other state?

A: Alaska

Key Words

climate: the average weather of an area over a period of time

drought: a period of time when it does not rain

hailstorm: a storm where small pieces of ice, called hail, fall from the sky

hemisphere: one of two halves of Earth, especially above or below the equator

humid: air that feels damp or moist on the skin

livestock: animals, such as cows and chickens, raised by farmers

orbits: travels around in a circle-like pattern

predict: to say that something will happen in the future

sunburn: damage to the skin from too much sunshine

thunderstorms: storms with lightning and thunder

weather satellites: vehicles in space that send information about weather back to Earth

Index

LIGHTBOX

SUPPLEMENTARY RESOURCES

Click on the plus icon ⊕ found in the bottom left corner of each spread to open additional teacher resources.

- Download and print the book's quizzes and activities
- Access curriculum correlations
- Explore additional web applications that enhance the Lightbox experience

LIGHTBOX DIGITAL TITLES
Packed full of integrated media

VIDEOS

INTERACTIVE MAPS

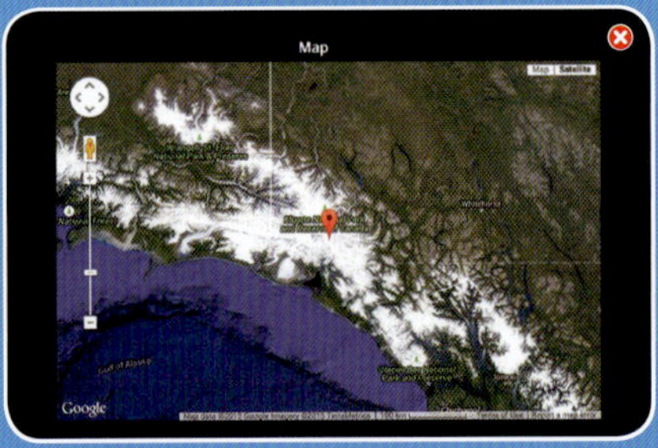

WEBLINKS

SLIDESHOWS

QUIZZES

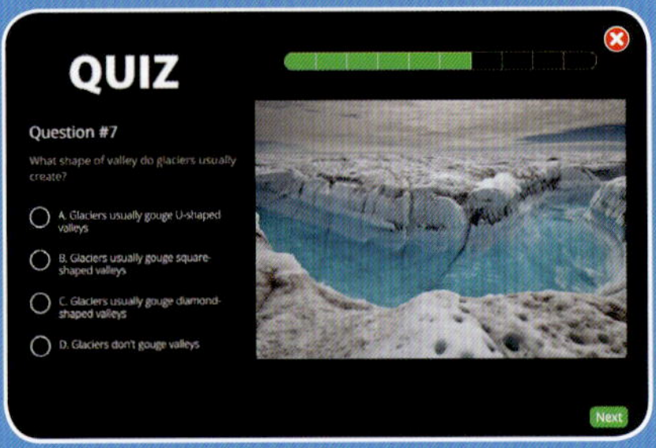

OPTIMIZED FOR

- ✔ TABLETS
- ✔ WHITEBOARDS
- ✔ COMPUTERS
- ✔ AND MUCH MORE!

Published by Smartbook Media Inc.
350 5th Avenue, 59th Floor New York, NY 10118
Website: www.openlightbox.com

Library of Congress Control Number: 2019942195

ISBN 978-1-5105-4518-2 (hardcover)
ISBN 978-1-5105-4519-9 (multi-user eBook)

Printed in Guangzhou, China
1 2 3 4 5 6 7 8 9 0 23 22 21 20 19

062019
122718

Project Coordinator: Priyanka Das
Designer: Ana María Vidal

Photo Credits
Every reasonable effort has been made to trace ownership and to obtain permission to reprint copyright material. The publisher would be pleased to have any errors or omissions brought to its attention so that they may be corrected in subsequent printings. The publisher acknowledges Getty Images, iStock, Shutterstock, and Alamy as its primary image suppliers for this title.